jF MONTGOME Anson
Your grandparents are
werewolves /
Montgomery, Anson,

CHOOSE YOUR OWN ADVENTURE®

Kids Love Reading
Choose Your Own Adventure®!

"Thank you for making these books for kids.
I bet kids that haven't read it yet would love it.
All I can say is that I love your books and I
bet other kids would love them too."
Bella Foster, age 8

"These books are really cool. When I get to
the end of the page, it makes me want to
keep going to find out what is going to happen
to me. I get to make my own choices of
what I WANT to happen next."
Bionca Samuel, age 10

"This book was good. I like that I got
to pick how the story went."
Lily von Trapp, age 7

"I like how you can make up the story,
but it also tells you a story."
Liam Stewart, age 8

"I like Choose Your Own Adventure more than normal books.
In a normal book I would have read two or three chapters
but instead I read three stories."
Soren Bay-Hansen, age 7

Illustrated by Keith Newton
Book design by Stacey Boyd, Big Eyedea Visual Design
For information regarding permission, write to:

CHOOSECO

P.O. Box 46, Waitsfield, Vermont 05673
www.cyoa.com

A DRAGONLARK BOOK

Published simultaneously in the United States and Canada

Printed in China

10 9 8 7 6 5 4 3 2 1

CHOOSE YOUR OWN ADVENTURE®

YOUR GRANDPARENTS ARE WEREWOLVES

BY ANSON MONTGOMERY

A DRAGONLARK BOOK

This book is dedicated to YOU! Keep on reading!

READ THIS FIRST!!!

WATCH OUT!
THIS BOOK IS DIFFERENT
from every book you've ever read.

Do not read this book from the first page through to the last page.
Instead, start on page 1 and read until you come to your first choice. Then turn to the page shown and see what happens.

When you come to the end of a story, you can go back and start again.
Every choice leads to a new adventure.

Good luck!

Tonight is the night! It's the first full moon of the year. Tonight you get to become a werewolf for the first time. You lie in bed all day waiting for the night to come.

"Try to get some sleep, honey," your mom says, closing the door to your room. "Grandma and Grandpa will be here soon. Dad and I have to go to the Monster Council meeting in Ghostburg. I can't believe my little baby will become a real werewolf tonight! *Sniff!*"

The door closes as you toss and turn.

You wake up in darkness. Two tall shapes stand over your bed. It's your grandparents, waking you up. It's werewolf time!

Grandma turns on the light and hands you a mug of hot cocoa.

"Drink up," she says, "you'll need it!"

"When do I change?" you ask, looking at your bare arms. When will they sprout hair and turn into paws like your grandparents' have? You can't wait!

"When the full moon rises, ten minutes from now. Don't worry, you'll know!" your grandma answers.

Turn to page 3.

You scramble to your paws, trying to avoid all the werewolves snapping at your sheep costume. But the more you struggle, the more they get excited.

"All right, pups," Gramp-wolf says, bounding onto the stage. "Enough of that foolishness!" he says, pulling the werewolves off you and then helping you up.

"I think all of you have had enough 'mutton' and more than enough 'moonlight' for the evening. How about you settle down and get ready for the next number?" Gramp-wolf says.

"Thank you, Gramp-wolf!" you say, suddenly tired and ready to go home.

The End

"What do you want to do tonight?" your grandma asks. "Grandpa is going to the Wolf School to help them get ready for the talent show against the Vampire Academy. It's lots of fun, and you'll get to meet the new kids in your Wolf School pack."

"That sounds fun," you say. "But what are you doing?"

"Some werewolves we know are getting stuck in between being a human and a werewolf. Wolf ears on a human head, or one hand and one paw. An old myth says the tooth of the First Werewolf might be the cure. I'm going to look," she says, jumping up and down in excitement. "It will be a night run, my favorite! The wind and the snow beneath your paws! There's nothing like it. Humans are so slow on their little stick legs."

Turn to the next page.

You look down at your hands. Your nails are growing right before your eyes! And hair is growing all over you. It itches! You scratch your ear with your left foot.

Your mouth starts to tickle. Then it stretches into a long muzzle. With a tilt of your head, you feel your ears grow upwards. You give them a little flick. It feel natural. In less than a minute, you are a werewolf! Your nose is long, your teeth are big and sharp, and you have a tail. You give it a swish. It's really fun.

"Arooooooo-ooooooo!" you howl in happiness. Both of your grandparents' fur goes up at your high-pitched wail.

"You need to work on that howl, kiddo," Grandpa says from the other side of the door. "So, what would you like to do? Werewolf School with me or join Grandma for a night run to look for the ancient tooth of the First Werewolf?"

If you choose to go to the Werewolf School and help set up for the talent show, turn to page 7

If you decide to look for the ancient tooth turn to page 11

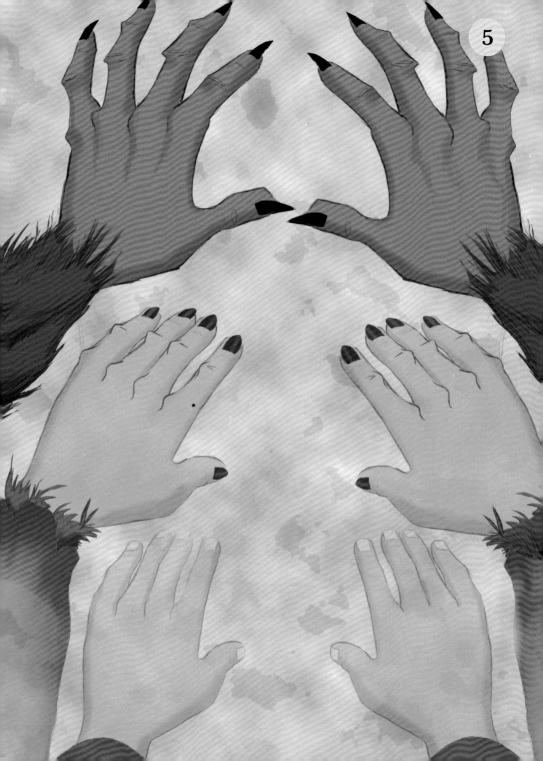

"C'mon, pup," your werewolf grandfather, or Gramp-wolf, says. "You're going to love Werewolf School. You're lucky to start right at the talent show, maybe you can even join in."

"Um, sorry, uh Gramp-wolf, but what *is* Werewolf School?" you ask.

"Well, you know how you go to human school to be a human?" he asks back.

"Yes, I guess," you say.

"Werewolf School is where you learn to be a werewolf. Learning things like howling, transforming, and learning to resist chicken coops," he explains. Then he adds in a whisper, "your Gram-wolf still needs to work on that one! Plus leaping and avoiding silver bullets, you know, werewolf stuff."

"Okay!" you agree, still not sure.

"Okay, let's go. The moon's just risen, so we have a little time before school starts!"

Gramp-wolf drives you to Wolf School in his regular car, but he drives with his head out of the window, letting his long tongue flap in the breeze. You try it. It's fun!

Turn to the next page.

You pull up to a big building with "Werewolf School: Making Wolves out of Pups since 1589." stitched on a banner. It's both spooky and welcoming. You're nervous, but inside it seems like a regular school. Regular except that everyone is a werewolf! Even the teachers and the janitor.

Gramp-wolf knows everyone and stops to talk to them all. He gets into a long, boring conversation about a plant called wolfsbane with one of the teachers.

"Hello, can you help me stack chairs for the talent show tonight?" a werewolf teacher with a conductor's baton asks. "We need to move them to the auditorium."

"Sure, I can help," you say.

Stacking the chairs is sort of fun, but not that fun. You aren't paying attention, and you drop a huge stack of chairs on your right back paw.

"YOWLLLL-AROOOOOO-GROOOLLLLL!!!" you howl in pain. "Aroooo-WOOOWOOOLOOOL!!!"

Turn to page 12

"Good choice, pup," Grandma says, scratching the back of your neck with her long claws. "Running is one of the great joys of being a werewolf!"

"Thanks for showing me, Grandma!" you say.

"Well, from now on, call me Gram-WOLF!"

With that, she bounds into the cold winter night.

Grandpa, or you guess, Gramp-wolf, turns to you and says, "Don't follow Gram if she chases any chickens! Especially avoid chicken coops!"

"Okay, Gramp-wolf!" you howl, chasing after Gram.

Running with Gram-wolf makes you jump in excitement. You skate across frozen lakes, glide through pine forests, and plow through whole snow drifts on your way to the top of the ridge.

"How are we going to find the ancient tooth to cure the werewolves stuck in between?" you ask when you reach the ridge. You pant with your tongue hanging out.

Turn to page 13.

The teacher just stares at you, then she says, "that is one of the most interesting howls I've ever heard! Can you do that again later tonight? You'd be perfect for the closing of *Howl Prowl!*"

"There you are, pup," Gramp-wolf says, coming over. "Want to check out the wolfball court? I used to be a pretty big player, back in the day! Should be fun to watch the team practice."

"We really could use your howling help," the music teacher wolf asks you. "No pressure but you are what we need to make it perfect!"

If you want to see the wolfball court with Gramp wolf and watch the team practice, turn to page 19

If you decide to help the music teacher by howling in the talent show later tonight turn to page 25

"We have to sneak into the hall of the Storm Giants. They know who has the tooth," Gram-wolf says, then she starts sniffing with her long, silver-furred nose. She rises up onto her hind legs and points to something down below you. "And that's how we'll get in! *SNIFF!*"

"Okay," you say, sniffing with your new nose. Now that you are paying attention you realize you can smell things that you never even knew had smells! But above it all, it stinks like two-week-old garbage.

Turn to the next page.

"It smells like old garbage," you say, not sure why Gram would lead you to it.

"Spot on," Gram-wolf says. "Let's go roll in it to hide our scent!"

"Okay," you say. You're excited, even though normally this would be way too gross. But now that you're a werewolf rolling in stinky garbage sounds fun!

"Okay, that should do it!" Gram-wolf says, giving one last hearty roll in the stinky mess before springing to all fours. "Now no one will know that two werewolves are nearby! Follow me!" Gram-wolf yells, shooting off into the night like a silver ghost.

Turn to page 16

You YELP! with excitement as you run after Gram-wolf. She leads you to the top of the ridge. It's hard keeping up with Gram-wolf, and your tongue steams in the freezing night air.

"Okay, kiddo, be very quiet from now on," she whispers into your ear. "Step where I step and try not to keep panting and slobbering like a Saint Bernard!"

Go on to the next page

Gram-wolf silently leaps from rock slabs to tree stumps, but then she slinks down when she reaches a clearing in the trees and inches through the snow.

You are following behind, as carefully as you can, when you hear a high-pitched cry. Even with your wolf hearing, it is very faint.

"Gram-wolf, wait up!" you say, stopping.

"Hurry up!" she says.

"Help! Mama! Help!" comes the voice.

"Did you hear that?" you ask, cocking your head to the side to try and figure out where it is coming from. Did you hear it or is it just the wind?

"No. We have to keep moving," she says, turning to go.

If you tell Gram-wolf to wait for you as you check it out, turn to page 38.

If you decide it was just the wind and continue to follow Gram-wolf, turn page 43.

You and Gramp-wolf head outside to the huge wolfball court. It's bigger than a football field, with trees and boulders on it and lots of colored lines. You've never seen a sports field like it before.

"Throw it to me!" a shaggy teen wolf yells to one of her teammates.

Another teen wolf, this one with dyed purple ears, takes a boulder and throws it over. You flinch, worried that the wolf is about to be knocked out, but she catches it in one paw, pulls back a pine tree with a basket tied to it, and uses it as a catapult to launch the rock at the other team. It knocks over one of the other team's wolf head rocks, and the members of the first team cheer.

"What's going on?" you ask Gramp-wolf.

"It's complicated. But let's just say one team is trying to knock over the other team's wolf head rocks by throwing rocks at them."

"Don't they get hurt?" you ask, seeing one wolf take a large rock in the belly.

"Werewolves are pretty tough," Gramp-wolf says. "Gentler games are no fun for us."

Turn to the next page.

The game of wolfball ends when the first team knocks over the last two heads. Afterwards, the team slap paws and tell each other "good game." One wolf, the shaggy one who knocked over one of the heads, comes over to you and Gramp-wolf.

"Wow, so glad you came to see us practice! You're 'Rock Thrower' Wolf, aren't you?" the shaggy wolf asks Gramp-wolf. "I'm honored to have you here! You're a legend!"

Gramp-wolf tries to look modest, but you can tell that he is pleased to be recognized.

"Actually, if you could show my Grand-pup how the game works, that would be wonderful."

Go on to the next page

"Sure thing," says the shaggy werewolf, smiling a big smile with lots of teeth. "My name's Anneka, and can show you how to play. But I'm also the guide from the welcoming committee. I'm supposed to show you around! We could fit in a little bit of wolfball practice or I could show you your new classroom and introduce you to your new teacher."

If you want to learn how to play wolfball with Anneka right now, turn to page 28.

If you've had enough wolfball and want to see your classroom and meet your teacher, turn to the next page.

Gramp-wolf looks a bit disappointed that you aren't going to learn how to play wolfball. But you really want to see your classroom and meet your new teacher.

"Come on," Anneka says, taking your paw and leading you back to the school building. "School's just about to start."

Werewolf students stream into the school's open doors. It could be an ordinary day, but it is night and you are a werewolf. It feels like a dream. Anneka takes you to a room in the back of the building. A werewolf teacher wearing a sport coat and a necktie stands at a desk at the front of the classroom.

"Mr. Loopin, this is your new student and grandfather wolf, old Rock Thrower from the school's wolfball hall of fame." Anneka says, introducing you.

"Great, nice to meet you. Can you help me put these bones on each student's desk? We're going to be going over proper bone-chewing technique. You have to be careful of splinters."

"I'll leave you here," Anneka says. "I've got to get to my own classroom."

Go on to the next page

Instead of a bell, class starts with a spooky, and
ɔud, howl through the school's speaker system.

"Welcome to our new student." Mr. Loopin says.
˙he other werewolves turn and stare at you. You feel
little nervous. But then they smile at you and say
hi."

"Today we'll be learning how to chew on bones and
ɪow to get rid of fleas."

You didn't notice before, but now that Mr. Loopin
ɪentioned fleas, you feel itchy all over.

Turn to the next page.

"You did a good job on your bone," Mr. Loopin says at the end of the night, "but you need to practice more to avoid getting splinters. Here's another bone. Please have it properly chewed by tomorrow night."

Your first night of Werewolf School and you have homework.

By the end of the school night, when the moon sets, you are exhausted.

The End

Mrs. Wolfgang is the choir teacher, and she is in charge of the singing part of the talent show. Right now it is looking like the show may NOT go on. You're supposed to make the same howl you did when you dropped the chair on your paw, but you can't get the right noise to come out.

All the other werewolves are muttering and looking at you sideways. Everyone is tired.

"Okay, how about this?" Mrs. Wolfgang says. "Instead of doing *Howl Prowl* we do *Mutton in the Moonlight*. Our new friend can play the role of the mutton."

"What's mutton?" you ask.

Everyone giggles and stares at you.

"It's an old sheep," Mrs. Wolfgang explains patiently. "All you have to do is stand there. In the moonlight, in the sheep costume."

Turn to the next page.

When you finally tuck your tail into the sheep costume, you feel very silly. The costume is so fluffy that you can barely move. You tell the choir teacher you don't like being a mutton.

"It's up to you. We could try *Howl Prowl,* but you have to really howl. *Mutton in the Moonlight* is a classic, everyone would really like that song!"

This is a lot of pressure. How did you end up the star of the show? You aren't even a student here yet.

If you'll wear the sheep costume and sing Mutton in the Moonlight, *turn to page 32*

If you think you can get that special howl, sing Howl Prowl *on page 34*

Wolfball is hard! Wolfball is fun!

Rocks hit you in the face, the back, and on your legs, but you don't really feel them. It hurts less than playing tag as a human. The feeling isn't much different than jumping in a cold lake.

"You!" Anneka says, pointing at you. "Take the catapult and tie it to the big pine tree straight ahead, we should be able to knock over their wolf head rocks from there."

You don't really know what you are doing, but you tie the catapult to the tree that Anneka is pointing at.

"Watch out!" someone yells, and you see that your legs are caught up in the ropes of the catapult. Then someone lets the tree go and you go flying through the air.

WHAM!

You crash into one of the wolf heads, and the breath is knocked from you.

Turn to page 30

You whimper like a pup for a bit, then you shake yourself and rush to the other wolf head. Pushing it over is hard, especially with the other team pushing against you, but you manage to get it knocked over.

"Come on, now let's tag up to settle the score!" Anneka yells.

You follow the other werewolves on your team and run to the far side of the wolfball court and tag up at the jail.

You still don't really understand the game, but you have a fun time laughing with the other players.

"Okay, time to wrap it up!" Anneka says. "School starts in ten minutes!"

By the end of the school night, you have made some friends and know your way around a little bit. Gramp-wolf takes you home before the moon sets. You were so tired out that you fell asleep during the talent show and missed it.

You can't wait to go back tomorrow night. Wolfball is cool! You hope you can be as good at it as Gramp-wolf someday.

The End

You watch the talent show from the back of the theater, and you get very nervous about your role as the *Mutton in the Moonlight.*

"Okay, werewolves, up next is the Wolf Choir singing *Mutton in the Moonlight.* Speaking of mutton, don't forget to buy some meat pies during intermission," the host tells the audience. Gramp-wol called your parents, and now they are sitting in the front row.

You wait in the wings while the other werewolf students file out onto stage, singing the new song. You didn't even have time to practice! What are you supposed to do?

Ohhh, the mutton in the moonlight
Such a tempting sight
But I must fight, the urge to bite
I need to wait for blackest night
Not here with all so bright
Such a long, tempting night
But I must continue to fight,
To fight the urge to BITE

Go on to the next page

The chorus of werewolves is really belting it out when you stumble onto the stage, dressed up like an old sheep. You freeze, not knowing what to do. You're right there, on stage in front of the whole school, an actual wolf in sheep's clothing.

They sing the chorus again, but this time, when they get to the final, "BITE!," all the werewolves on stage pounce on you and tear the sheep costume to pieces. You get nipped a couple of times.

The whole auditorium goes nuts! A couple of young werewolves jump on the stage and start biting at you.

You are scared! Some of the bites hurt, even through the costume. Should you play dead or run backstage?

If you don't want to risk getting bitten any more and want to run backstage, turn to page 2.

If you decide to play dead and hope the werewolves stop biting you, turn to page 36.

The auditorium is dark, and you are nervous. You are up next! How can you get back the howl that made Mrs. Wolfgang put you in the talent show?

"All right, a big round of applause for the amazing acrobatics of the Wonderful Wolf Women." the host of the talent show says. A big round of applause comes from the crowd. So far you have seen a werewolf jump through rings of fire, a couple of vampires dancing as bats with silver streamers coming off their wings, and a zombie who mumbled a few things and then left a foot on stage. The choir goes on stage, and right before you join them, you see one of the sandbags that hold down the curtains. You hide it under your robes and scurry onto stage with the other members of the choir.

Everything seems like a blur as you sing *Howl Prowl.*

Go on to the next page

"And then you howl!! When you're on the prowl!" This time, you drop the sandbag on your paw, and with a huge scream, you give the best howl of your life:

AROOOOOOO-OOOOWWWWW!!

Howl Prowl doesn't win the talent show, but Mrs. Wolfgang is happy, and so are you!

The End

"Ouch!" you cry, as the werewolves bite at you through the costume. It hurts. But you stay as still as you can, curled up in a ball on the stage.

"Stop it! Stop it!" yells Mrs. Wolfgang, and everyone calms down. She helps you offstage and then helps you out of the sheep costume. Luckily you are okay. But it was scary.

Then you hear cheering and clapping.

"Go on," Mrs. Wolfgang says. "Time to take your bows."

You go back onstage and the crowd goes crazy again.

"How about that!" says the announcer. "I think we have a winner."

Go on to the next page

You are the celebrity of the school, and everyone
wants to show you what makes Werewolf School the
best. Anneka offers to take you to see Gramp-wolf's
trophy for wolfball.

"What's your favorite class?" you ask her.

"Science! Definitely science," she says. "We could
go meet the science teacher if you want?"

If you want to go to science class, turn to page 55.

If you want to see Gramp-wolf's trophy,
turn to page 57.

"I think there's something out there that needs help, Gram-wolf." you tell her, feeling deep down that you are right. "Let's *really* listen this time."

"Okay," she says. "I'm not sure these old ears are as sharp as yours! I didn't hear anything before."

"Shush!" you say to Gram-wolf. She gives you a cold stare. A cold werewolf stare.

"Help!"

"Did you hear that?" you ask.

"Nope, and don't 'shush' your Gram-wolf."

"Mama, help me Mama!"

"Over there!" you say, listening to the wind. "It's coming from that way."

You go deep into the dark woods. No moonlight makes it in. But you don't need moonlight to see.

"Mama!"

"I heard it that time." Gram-wolf says. "Let's pick up the pace."

Go on to the next page

"HELP Meeeee! Ar-rooooooo!"

You reach a small clearing and in the middle, bathed in the glow from the full moon, is a baby werewolf. Tears are frozen on his furry cheeks and he is howling at the moon.

"Ar-roooOOOOOO!" Gram-wolf howls, joining in. The baby werewolf looks over at you and smiles.

Turn to the next page.

"Mama! Mama! I'm a big pup! Mama!" the baby werewolf says, breaking into sobs again.

"I think he wants his mama," you say. "Hey buddy. We'll find your mama. It's okay."

He stops crying again. Gram-wolf nods her head at you to say "good job."

"Okay. Good. We'll find your mama for you. What's her name?"

"Mama!" the baby werewolf says, looking at you like you are crazy.

"Yes, of course. What's your name? Do you know that?"

Go on to the next page

"I'm a sweet pup," he says, sounding only fairly ure about that.

"We should take him to town," Gram-wolf says. We don't want him to catch cold, and they'll know jhat to do with him."

"But what if his mama is nearby?" you ask. "Don't ɹe want to at least just look around?"

If you want to take the baby werewolf to town,
turn to page 49.

If you think you should look around first,
turn to page 64.

Gram-wolf leads you to
a bunch of flat rocks, each
swept clear of snow.
A group of monster kids
and their friends and parents
sit there with picnic baskets.
A Frankenstein family is
trying to quiet the Franken-
baby.

Turn to the next page.

Gram-wolf leaps high in the air from the forest, landing in the middle of the rocks. The monsters all look up, but none seem surprised.

"Hi, Eugenia," the Franken-mom says to Gram-wolf, bouncing the baby in the air. "Any tips on getting this little monster to calm down?"

"Weren't you surprised by my entrance?" Gram-wolf says, a little let down that they aren't screaming in terror.

"The Zombies aren't in town, who else would smell like rotten garbage?" asks the Mommy mummy, laughing. Gram-wolf bares her teeth, just a little.

"Anyway, let me introduce you to my Grand-pup."

The little vampire motions you over. He has a fancy cape and a little black bow tie with a gold medallion on a chain.

Go on to the next page

"Hi, my name's Vammy," he says, putting out his pale hand. "Shake?" he asks, laughing. His hand is very cold.

"This is my friend Sammy," he says, turning to the little mummy.

Sammy has a cookie in its mouth, so it just mumbles, "Hi!"

Turn to the next page.

"Want to join us for a snack?" Vammy asks, pointing to the blanket with sandwiches, fizzy drinks, and cookies.

"Sure," you say, making sure Gram-wolf nods that it's okay. Vammy and Sammy are really fun and the food is delicious. Vammy's dad even finds a big bone for you to chew on! You've never loved the taste of a bone so much in your life.

Go on to the next page

Just as you are finishing your midnight picnic, Gram-wolf brings up your mission to find the ancient tooth.

"It's a big nuisance," Gram-wolf explains. "I know it is kind of funny seeing someone with a wolf's nose on a human face, unless it happens to you! Do you know if the Storm Giants have the ancient tooth?"

"The Storm Giants probably know where it is, or was, but I doubt they have it," the vampire mom says as she helps pack up the midnight picnic. "The Lake Monster may know. She's been around since before there were werewolves. She'll be at the Moon Ceremony later tonight."

If you choose to go ask the Lake Monster if she knows, turn to page 61.

If you want to visit the Storm Giants to ask them if they have the tooth, turn to page 68.

"We need to take this werewolf pup to Monster-Town, it is too cold and he could get sick," you tell Gram-wolf.

"I think you're right," Gram-wolf says. "And the fastest way to town from up this high on the ridge is by taking the ice slide."

"Do you think that's safe?" you ask. An ice slide sounds scary.

"We don't have time to worry about that. Follow me!" Gram-wolf yells, picking up the werewolf pup and diving headfirst down the ice slide to Monster-Town.

In a flash she is gone, with a swirl of snow left behind her.

You take a deep breath and follow her.

The snow and ice get in your eyes, whiskers, and mouth. You can't see a thing! Using your claws and even your teeth, you are able to steer and slow yourself a little bit.

WHOOSH–SLAM!

Turn to the next page.

You crash into Gram-wolf at the bottom of the ice slide. The werewolf pup is covered in ice shavings. He sneezes on your face. Yuck!

"Watch it, pups," Gram-wolf says, laughing.

"I'm glad you enjoyed the slide to Monster-Town," a stern, deep voice says, not sounding glad at all. "Please present the licenses for these two underage werewolves, or face going to the pound!"

You look up to see a small gnome with Monster Police on his armband. He carries a whistle and a clipboard and wears a peaked cap with a shining silver star. You cringe back from the silver, letting loose a little growl.

Turn to page 52

"Easy, pup," Gram-wolf whispers. "It's my fault, I should have remembered that you need a license to enter town as a wolf. Ever since that *ONE* biting incident, now *ALL* werewolves have to have licenses."

Maybe you could take the pup and run for it?

"Don't think about it, wolf-child, I'm a skilled tracker," the gnome warns you. "Make a run for it and you'll regret it!"

If you think going to the Monster Pound is the better choice, turn to page 58

If you decide to make a break for it and run away from the Monster Police, turn to page 67

Your parents gave you a cell phone, just for emergencies, but you have a few games and apps on it. You scroll through trying to think of something that the giants would want.

"How about something that can tell you the weather?" you ask the Storm Giant King. You open your weather app and show them the weather report.

"Cloudy with a chance of showers Thursday, winds 20-30 miles per hour…"

"Deal," the Giant King says, throwing a tiny speck from his palm.

Gram-wolf snatches it from the air as it falls.

"Nice work, pup!" Gram-wolf says. "Let's go help the werewolves who are stuck in between."

The End

"Welcome to Wolf Science!" the feisty young teacher, Mr. W. Bane, tells the class. He is a dark werewolf, with a long streak of white fur running down his back. "Today we're playing with fire, silver, and other dangerous-to-werewolves items. Please treat it all carefully!"

Mr. Bane puts on a leather glove over his paw. He takes out a vial filled with silver liquid and places it on the table.

"Do we have a volunteer?"

Without thinking, you raise your paw.

"Good! We have a brave pup here," Mr. Bane says. "This won't hurt...much, or at least not for very long."

He pours the silver liquid over your head.

It burns and your fur falls out wherever you were touched by it.

Your fur grows back white wherever it touched. Now you are a spotted werewolf.

The End

"Here we are!" Anneka says, showing you a dark all with statues of werewolves wearing spacesuits, uits of armor, and regular suits like politicians wear.

"Who knew there were so many famous and nportant werewolves?" you say, looking at all of the xhibits. There are animatronic werewolves talking bout the Great Vampire Peace Act and the founding f Monster-Town.

"See, without the werewolves, Monster-Town rouldn't even exist!" Anneka says. You are so tired om the full night of excitement. Before you know , you are curled in a little ball of fur on the floor, noring and snuffling in your sleep. Anneka tries to vake you up, but you don't budge and finally she ives up and falls asleep next to you.

The End

"Come along then," the gnome says, taking a gold chain as thin as a human hair and tying your hands together.

Go on to the next page

"I'll get your parents," Gram-wolf tells you with fake heerfulness. "We'll get it all sorted out. Including nding this little guy's mama."

"You know, having a license is for your own good," ne gnome says. "Trust me, I don't like putting young nonsters in the pound."

You think he is lying. He seems to enjoy it quite a ot.

You are taken to a dark cell in the pound, and just s you are about to be thrown in, the police gnome rings you out front. There is a beautiful werewolf vith a silver streak of fur on her head.

"There's my baby!" she says. "I have the paperwork or little Oscar's license right here. You can just add he license for the other werewolf as well."

"Thank you," you say.

"Your grandmother found me as I made my way ack from the forest," the werewolf mother says. Thank you for taking care of my little pup."

The End

"Hurry up and shake four legs before the Moon Ceremony starts!" Gram-wolf says, bounding away from the picnic rocks.

After an hour of running, Gram-wolf stops at a huge frozen lake. The ice is so clear you can see down into the reeds and lilies. You step on the ice with just one paw, and it is solid. Following Gram-wolf, you slip and slide on the ice. You use your claws to dig in, leaving white scratch marks on the smooth surface.

In the middle of the lake, a spring bubbles, breaking a hole in the ice. Rabbits, bears, mice, eagles, bluejays, and more crowd around the spring. The water churns faster, and then a long, colorful sea-serpent rises out of the hole, splashing you with freezing lake water. All the animals let out yells of happiness and surprise at being splashed, and you join in!

Turn to the next page.

The Lake Monster settles her long head on the ice, and the animals crowd around her, telling and asking her things in their different languages.

Finally it is your turn! You face the lake monster.

"I need to find the First Wolf's tooth. I need it to help my werewolf friends who are stuck between human and wolf."

"I do know where one of the First Wolf's teeth is."

"Where?" you ask.

"It's at the bottom of this lake, lost in the mud. It cracked off when the First Wolf tried to bite a fish in the water. She broke her tooth off on the ice! Then it fell to the bottom."

"Can you get it for us?"

"Sorry, but it is lost in the mud!"

With that, the Lake Monster raises her head towards the moon, then dives back into the hole in the ice and disappears.

The End

"Okay, little guy, where's your mama?" you ask him gently.

"MAMA!" he wails.

"Where'd she go?"

Gram-wolf picks up the werewolf pup before he can cry again, and she snuggles him close. He sighs and snuggles back.

"Mama," he moans.

You search the little opening in the woods. You see a lot of your and Gram-wolf's paw prints, but you also see a few large prints off to the south. But there aren't any more prints after that. Where did she go?

"Look over there!" you yell, pointing to a large pine tree that doesn't have any snow on it like the others do. There's a big pile of snow at the base of the tree. "She's in there! Under the snow!"

You, Gram-wolf, and even the little werewolf pup ig and dig to get his mom out from under the huge ile of snow.

She struggles up out of the snow, and coughs and neezes a bunch.

The baby werewolf yells, "Mama!" and leaps to nuggle in with his mom.

"Oscar, come to Mama. Thanks so much for igging me out of that snow pile," the mama verewolf says, licking Oscar's face with her tongue. You are heroes for saving me!"

"It was mostly my Grand-pup here!" Gram-wolf ays, smiling at you. "You are the real hero!"

The End

You leap to your four paws, grab the werewolf pup, and bound away from the ice slide. You are fast! In just a few seconds you are far away, heading down the narrow streets of Monster-Town. You turn a corner and catch your breath out of sight.

A zombie wearing a hat with a flower says, "I saw you run for it, pup. Don't waste your time, Officer Gnomler takes his job serious. He'll catch you!"

You push on, looking for something to hide your scent from the tracker.

Then you see Officer Gnomler across the main plaza. He is riding a chicken with a saddle and spurs. You run again, this time not stopping until you are far out of town. But as soon as you stop, you see the gnome on his war-chicken. Getting closer!

Finally you are too tired to run and Officer Gnomler catches up to you and hands you a ticket.

"Now you can't get a license for three months," Gnomler says, looking pleased. "And you have to pay a fine of one million monster-bucks!"

"Mama!! Hungry!" wails the werewolf pup. You still need to find the pup's mom and now he's hungry!

The End

The run to the Hall of the Storm Giant King makes you bone-tired.

"Okay, pup, we made it," Gram-wolf says, finally stopping in front of a huge stone cliff.

A tall doorway opens to a hall that is warm and full of light. Giants eat and talk at a giant-sized table. Storm clouds circle their massive heads, and zaps of lightning make their hair stand on end.

Turn to the next page.

A normal, human-sized staircase rises ten flights of stairs to the table, where a little podium with a megaphone is set up.

"More steps!" you groan, looking at the staircase.

"Yup!" Gram-wolf says, sprinting up it. You follow
ehind. Stairs are not easy for wolves to climb.

When Gram-wolf gets to the megaphone, she leans
1 and yells as loud as she can.

"Greetings, Storm King, I've come to ask a
uestion!"

"Greetings, Eugenia," the Storm Giant King roars
ack. You feel the words ripple through your whole
ody like a hand shaking you. "What is the question?"

"Do you know where the ancient tooth of the First
Verewolf is?" your grandmother asks.

"Yes, but the answer will cost you!"

"I wish he would whisper," you whisper to Gram-
volf.

The Storm Giant King hears what you say. "This *is*
ny whisper!" he booms. "If you want the tooth, you
ave to give something of equal value!"

Gram-wolf turns to you and shrugs. She whispers:
Do you have anything to give him?"

Turn to page 53.

ABOUT THE ARTIST

Keith Newton began his art career in the theater as a set painter. Having talent and a strong desire to paint portraits, he moved to New York and studied fine art at the Art Students League. Keith has won numerous awards in art such as The Grumbacher Gold Medallion and Salmagundi Award for Pastel. He soon began illustrating and was hired by Disney Feature Animation where he worked on such films as *Pocahontas* and *Mulan* as a background artist. Keith also designed color models for sculptures at Disney Animal Kingdom and has animated commercials for Euro Disney. Today, Keith Newton freelances from his home and teaches entertainment illustration at The College for Creative Studies in Detroit. He is married and has two daughters.

ABOUT THE AUTHOR

After graduating from Williams College with a degree specialization in ancient history, **Anson Montgomery** spent ten years founding and working in technology-related companies, as well as working as a freelance journalist for financial and local publications. He is the author of a number of books in the original *Choose Your Own Adventure* series, including *Everest Adventure, Snowboard Racer, Moon Quest* (reissued in 2008 by Chooseco), and *CyberHacker* as well as two volumes of *Choose Your Own Adventure: The Golden Path.* Anson lives in Warren, Vermont, with his wife, Rebecca, and his two daughters, Avery and Lila.

For games, activities, and other fun stuff, or to write to Anson Montgomery, visit us online at www.cyoa.com